e

on

ᴄᴏ ᴍᴀᴋɪɴɢ ᴀ ᴘɪᴌɢʳⁱᵐᵃᵍᵉ ·· · ·
Island of Lindisfarne.

We have included prayers and activities
to help you focus on your journey
whether your pilgrimage is part of your
inward journey or a physical journey to a
sacred place.

With every blessing,

Mary and Mark Fleeson
Holy Island

The
Creative Pilgrimage
ACTIVITY BOOK
by
Mary and Mark Fleeson
with
Clive Price

PRAYER
for a
PILGRIM

Be by my side Creator God,

Every step I take,

Be before me Saviour God,

Every step I take,

Be behind me Merciful God,

Every step I take,

Be within me Strengthening God

Every step I take.

Pilgrimage: The Inward and Outward Journey.

Anyone with children will be familiar with the phrase, 'Are we nearly there yet?' It will usually be heard five minutes into a journey and be repeated at regular intervals in a whiny tone guaranteed to grate on the most patient of companions.

The demands of everyday life often propel us into a way of existing that is contrary to our human nature, we need a balance of work, rest, play and spiritual growth but we rush from one activity to the next squeezing in moments of rest and non-work pursuits but rarely stopping, really stopping, to assess where we are and whether we want to be there. We seldom give ourselves time to discover where we are in our relationship with God, with our family and friends or who we have become as the years have sped by. Our life journeys become frustrated and tiring and our weary souls begin the cry, 'Am I nearly there yet?'

Pilgrimage is an opportunity to review those things from the focus of a God-centred journey.

I have always thought of pilgrimage as encompassing two distinct and yet complementary concepts, the physical journey to a spiritually significant place and the journey of the heart and mind as they move nearer to God. In the first case we make a choice to travel somewhere because we believe that the journey will be beneficial to our spiritual and emotional growth and being at the destination will bring us closer to God's blessing and deeper understanding of our Creator.

The journey of the heart and mind is a different process, we are all on this pilgrimage, not by choice but because we live. The only control we have over it is to decide how we travel, do we go willingly with an open heart, an open mind and the discipline to make time to withdraw from the rush and busyness of life so that we can take in the view and glimpse the road ahead, or do we allow ourselves to be pushed along, stopping only occasionally to glance back at where we've been?

"PILGRIMAGE ENCOMPASSES TWO DISTINCT AND YET COMPLEMENTARY CONCEPTS, THE PHYSICAL JOURNEY TO A SPIRITUALLY SIGNIFICANT PLACE AND THE JOURNEY OF THE HEART AND MIND AS THEY MOVE NEARER TO GOD".

Where are you headed today?

If you have brought this book with you as you travel on a pilgrimage to a particular place then spend regular times in silence, listening not only to the sounds around you but to all that the journey and the place wants to tell you.

Seek God in the ordinary, you may be experiencing an extraordinary journey or destination but the time you have set aside for a pilgrimage gives an ideal opportunity to be aware of the creativity and grace of God.

Perhaps you are at home and exploring the idea of pilgrimage, you may not be able to venture out to a far-flung place at this time. The practices are the same, listen - God speaks all the time, through our experiences, through nature, through others.

Seek God in the ordinary day to day things of daily living, look at the things you do, the people you interact with and the hum-drum daily activities with fresh eyes, ask God to help you to see with His eyes, hear with His ears and act with grace and love.

May my conversations be significant,
May my meetings be blessed,
May my path cross the paths of others who love You.
May my path cross the paths of others who don't know You
May my touch be Your touch of infinite gentleness,
May my words be Your words of wisdom,
May my eyes see with Your compassion.

On a traditional pilgrimage the pilgrim makes a journey to a place of spiritual importance; the journey is a time of reflection and of self sacrifice. The goal is to gain a greater understanding of God and self, to find healing, to atone for sins and to experience something of the atmosphere or 'spirit' that has made the destination special. Many people travel to Holy Island seeking that sense of the extraordinary, the feeling that God is so close that you only have to reach out your hand and you will feel a warm, strong hand pulling you nearer; the feeling that your prayers are somehow reinforced by all the prayers of those who have worshipped there before; the feeling that is like the anticipation of a wonderful promise about to be fulfilled.

The experience is very real, unique to each person and yet if acknowledged, will have the same result — a revelation of God's presence in that person's life and an encouragement that the Holy Spirit around us is in close communication with the Spirit within us.

"The first time I travelled across the causeway onto the Island of Lindisfarne I wept uncontrollably, I had only a little knowledge of the place and its history, I wasn't on a pilgrimage and I'm not particularly given to over-emotional outbursts, but I wept as though I had come home after being away for a lifetime." (Mary)

I have heard many similar stories over the last few years and the experience is always hard to put into words; you know you should be able to hold and see 'it' because 'it' feels so real but 'it' is intangible and may not be sensed by everyone or experienced in the same way.

When you embark on any journey it helps to be prepared, a map might not be essential if you are happy to surrender to the excitement of a mystery tour but if you don't keep everyone around you occupied, or at the very least content, then every time you stop to admire the view or relax into the pleasure of travelling you will hear the timeless phrase, 'Are we nearly there yet?' or 'I'm bored.'

It is the same when you embark on an inward pilgrimage, the times of spiritual growth require the discipline of separation, quiet and calm.

Perhaps you are travelling to a place where a particular Godly person was known to live, try asking that person a question or imagining how they might have responded to a situation you find yourself in OR ask yourself what would Jesus have said or done OR imagine how a favourite writer or disciple might respond. In imagining we are not expecting them to suddenly reply but attempting to see situations from another perspective.

Turn off the TV or radio, turn the ringer off the phone, occupy the family and forget the chores - even if it is only for a few minutes. The stages of your journey will need to be tailored to the time you have, if you only have ten minutes then you won't have time to do any lengthy preparation to get you into a 'good place', so light a candle or find a picture which inspires or comforts you, take a few deep breaths, say a prayer, perhaps the Jesus Prayer, "Lord Jesus Christ, Son of God, have mercy on me."

Then be silent.

If worries of the day enter your mind repeat the prayer and focus your eyes on the candle or image. You could ask God a question or you could just rest and be open to hearing His words. If you have longer then listening to instrumental music may be helpful, or colouring in, or meditating on a passage of the Bible.

The aim is to deliberately enter into the presence of God, to follow Him willingly wherever He leads.

That glorious, overwhelming sense of arriving and connecting with a place is not confined to a physical environment or moment in time, God is right beside you now, reaching out His warm hand and waiting for you to hold it; the supplication of the Saints who lived before surround us with a blanket of prayers that join with ours, because the God who hears them is outside our linear concept of time; His wonderful promise is fulfilled when we accept the Holy Spirit as our guide and helper in this pilgrimage of life.

On the following pages
are some prayers to help you
focus through the day.

PRAYERS for the MORNING

May each moment today
be filled with light,
May each challenge today
be met with grace,
May each choice today follow Your plan
And may I sense Your wondrous presence in all.

Thank you for this new day and for holding me safe through the night.

Thank you for this new day
Help me to live in Your presence
And to recognize You in those I meet.

Thank you for this new day
Help me to hear the silent cries
Of those you have equipped me to help.

Thank you for this new day.

PRAYERS for the MIDDLE of the DAY

Help me Dear Lord, to care too much,
to love too freely, to pray unceasingly,
to forgive endlessly, to laugh fearlessly,
to question, to live, to be who I am,
to be where I am, to be what I am,
to hope, to believe, to reach out my hand.

May this moment, right now, radiate peace,
Like a pebble thrown in still water,
May my being in Your presence
Spread Your love to those around me
And throughout the remainder of the day.

In the midst of this day let me not be so busy
That Your voice is lost.

In the midst of this day let me not be so tired
That Your will is not done.

In the midst of this day let me find peace
And time to just be.

AS AIDAN CARED FOR THE SOULS OF OTHERS,
HELP ME TO LOVE UNCONDITIONALLY.
AS CUTHBERT TRUSTED IN YOU FOR ALL HIS NEEDS,
HELP ME TO HAVE FAITH.
AS EADFRITH WAS INSPIRED TO GLORIFY YOU,
HELP ME TO BE CREATIVE.
AS THIS ISLAND HAS BEEN SOAKED IN PRAYER,
HELP ME TO PRAY UNCEASINGLY.

PRAYERS for the NIGHT

I bind my mind to the mind of the Creator God
and I loose from my mind all that offends my God.
That I may worship completely.
I bind my body to the will of the Saviour Christ
and I loose from my body all dis-ease.
That I may serve Freely.
I bind my spirit to the Holy Spirit my helper
and I loose from my spirit all that is not of my God.
That I may love joyfully...

Circle me this night,
Keep peace within
and anger without.

Circle me this night,
Keep comfort within
and hardship without.

Circle my home this night,
Keep safety within
and danger without.

My life is in Your hands,
hold me gently as I rest.

As I breathe in I give thanks
for the day now ending.

As I breathe out I place into
Your hands the things left
unfinished.

As I breathe in I pray
for Your blessing
on those who love You.

Take my beginnings
and bless their completion,

Take my striving
and soften their need,

Take my journey
and lead me deeper.

As I breathe out I pray
for Your blessing
on those who don't know You.

Come away to Lindisfarne.

For Holy Island has a place for you. There are many paths on this sacred isle. The first takes you across the sands at low tide. The next one takes you to a secluded beach or cosy bar. Yet another takes you to castle or kiln.

Whoever you are, whatever your background, you can follow your own path on this isle. You might be pilgrim or tourist, leader or follower, employed or retired, teacher or student. There is a way marked out for you.

Many choose to take off their shoes and walk to this monastic isle. They cross the one-and-a-half mile stretch of sand, while the sea waits in the distance. Everyone is on a journey on Holy Island.

Twice a day, this place is isolated from the mainland by a tidal channel. Twice a day, you have the opportunity to feel separated from your fears and concerns, while you enjoy the peace and tranquility of this place.

The weather will take you by surprise. For one minute you can be walking down rain-drenched streets. And the next minute you can be strolling along sun-soaked sands. This is the land of big, open skies.

While on your journey around Lindisfarne, think of it also like opening a book. The causeway and sands are the dramatic opener to this island saga. The ancient streets, priory ruins and restored castle offer romantic stories. The sea is a constant dialogue.

Or you could approach the island like studying a grand painting. This timeless tapestry spans before you with solid markers on the horizon, the castle and the land. But the backdrop of sky and sea changes every day, sometimes every moment.

And what is the content of this book, this work of art? There is the nuts-and-bolts story of industry on this island, the sweat and grind of the lime kilns and the fishing boats. There is the bravery of those who saved lives at sea.

There are also the daring exploits of other Holy Island heroes like Aidan and Cuthbert. These inspiring figures from antiquity helped bring Christian civilisation to Northern England. Walk the paths they walked. Breathe the air they breathed.

Aidan came here from Iona in the seventh century. Now his statue stands unmoved by time. For this place has eternal qualities. Mysterious as the mist, overwhelming as the ocean, Lindisfarne reaches into your soul.

From its monastic traditions to its herring fishing, the island offers reflection and reality. From the mudflats to the causeway, it's a small site with a vast, open setting. There is beauty and depth here.

Come away to Lindisfarne.

MANY OF US HAVE A FAVOURITE PLACE, SOMEWHERE SPECIAL THAT HELPS US TO FEEL CLOSER TO GOD.

CONSIDER WHAT IT IS THAT MAKES A PLACE LIKE THAT, IS IT THAT IT INSPIRES YOU? CHALLENGES YOU? MAKES YOU FEEL PEACEFUL?

ARE THERE WAYS THAT YOU COULD BRING THOSE ATTRIBUTES HOME? COULD YOU SHARE THEM WITH OTHERS?

Every year on Lindisfarne people build little towers of stones on the shoreline, they may represent prayers or people or the visit itself. It can be helpful to remember an event or a place by collecting pebbles or similar objects then displaying them at home. Pebbles could be stacked and each one assigned to a prayer, perhaps for the place and the people where they came from, the place and the people where they now are and one to commit your journey through life, to the God who created you.

Visiting the Holy Island of Lindisfarne

Holy Island is situated halfway between Newcastle and Edinburgh, just off the coast. It is a tidal Island which is accessible twice a day, please check the tide times at: www.northumberlandlife.org/holy-island

by Car: Follow the A1 and turn off at Beal, the turning is well signposted.

by Train: The nearest station is at Berwick-upon-Tweed, from there you will probably need to get a taxi as buses are few and far between.

by Air: The nearest Airports are Newcastle and Edinburgh.

Staying on the Island

Holy Island is home to several Retreat Houses and many other types of holiday accommodation.

Marygate House is an ecumenical Retreat House, it offers full board and operates on a donation basis.
For more information please visit:
www.marygatehouse.org.uk or call + 44 (0)1289 - 389246

The Open Gate is the Mother House of The Community of Aidan and Hilda, an ecumenical new monastic community which draws inspiration from the Celtic Saints, it offers B&B, organised, private and silent retreats and spiritual direction if needed. For more information please visit:
www.aidanandhilda.org.uk
or call + 44 (0)1289 389222

The Bothy at The St. Cuthbert's Centre is self catering. For more information please visit:
www.holyisland-stcuthbert.org
or call
+ 44 (0)1289 389254

For other accommodation please visit www.lindisfarne.org.uk

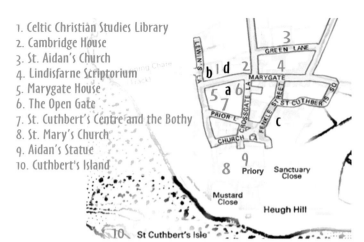

1. Celtic Christian Studies Library
2. Cambridge House
3. St. Aidan's Church
4. Lindisfarne Scriptorium
5. Marygate House
6. The Open Gate
7. St. Cuthbert's Centre and the Bothy
8. St. Mary's Church
9. Aidan's Statue
10. Cuthbert's Island

Also look out for, The Lindisfarne Centre (a) which has a facsimile of the Lindisfarne Gospels and fascinating exhibitions; The Post Office (b) everything you could want from a Village P.O. and delicious food too; The Island Store (c) groceries, ice-creams, gifts and more; The Gospel Garden (d), a peaceful place to relax. There's a great choice of gift shops, eateries, accommodation and attractions on Lindisfarne.

The Celtic Christian Studies Library (1) has been formed by the Community of Aidan and Hilda (see the map for the location) it is open to the public Mon. to Sat. between 10 am and 6 pm. For more information please visit: **www.aidanandhilda.org.uk**

'we have three vows. These are SIMPLICITY, PURITY and OBEDIENCE'
Community of Aidan and Hilda

Northumbria Community is a new monastic dispersed community with an identity rooted in the history and spiritual heritage of Celtic Northumbria. The Community has produced some wonderful resources for using on retreat and at home and it also has a Retreat House south of Holy Island on the Mainland. For more information please visit: **www.northumbriacommunity.org**

'The Rule we embrace and keep will be that of AVAILABILITY and VULNERABILITY.'
Northumbria Community

If you visit the Island please pray
for those who live here,
for those who work here,
for those who visit today,
for God's blessing on all.

Perhaps you will discover Aidan's statue?

Sun on the water, silver-gold ripples
bravely bright against
the slate-grey waves.

Did you see that same cold sea?
hear the birdsong of yesteryear?
the call of the seals?

Did you bow your head in the wind?
watch the grasses bend alongside?
the tide creeping in?

Did you sense the wondrous presence?
God worshipped at the thin place?
creating Holiness.

Or visit Cuthbert's Island

Born to be a warrior, to fight,
To dirty his hands in battle,
To take life, to stop the enemy.

Re-born to be a warrior, to fight,
To bare his soul as he prays,
To preach life, to stop the enemy.

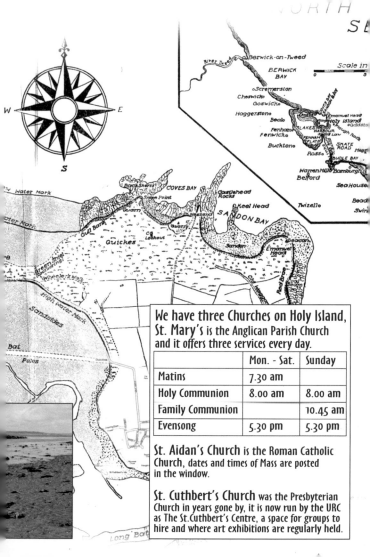

Berwick-on-Tweed
Scale in
0   5
BERWICK BAY
River Tweed
Scremerston
Cheswicke
Goswicke
Haggerstone
Beale
Fenham
Fenwicke
FENHAM FLATS
SLAKES
HARBOUR
Emanuel Head
Holy Island
Goldstone
Snake Law
Bucktone
SNAKE ROAD
Rosse
BUDLE BAY
Bamburgh
Meg
Warren Mill
Belford
Sea House
Twizelle
Beac
Swin

Water Mark
BLACK SKERRS
COVES BAY
Castlehead Rocks
Time Point
Keel Head
SANDON BAY
ter Mark
Gut Bank
Swan
Nessend
Quarry
Quickes
Lookout
Sanker
Beacon
Emanuel Head
Green Shiel
Wheelerton
Red Barns
High Water Mark
Sandridges
Bat
Poles
St. Cuthbert's Isle
Long Bat

We have three Churches on Holy Island,
St. Mary's is the Anglican Parish Church and it offers three services every day.

	Mon. - Sat.	Sunday
Matins	7.30 am	
Holy Communion	8.00 am	8.00 am
Family Communion		10.45 am
Evensong	5.30 pm	5.30 pm

St. Aidan's Church is the Roman Catholic Church, dates and times of Mass are posted in the window.

St. Cuthbert's Church was the Presbyterian Church in years gone by, it is now run by the URC as The St.Cuthbert's Centre, a space for groups to hire and where art exhibitions are regularly held.

Hints and tips for your inward and outward Pilgrimage

Take time out. Just ten minutes a day or half an hour twice a week set aside purely for being in God's presence can make a big difference to how your spiritual life grows. Find a quiet place and give the time you have to God, you could use one of the prayers in this book.

Pray like it's as vital as breathing. Sometimes we place praying, like God, into a box. We think God can only be met or talked to in Church or when a certain person is present, in reality we were created to communicate with our Creator, to enjoy a two-way conversation which never ends. There's so much God wants to share with us, to show us and teach us, so pray constantly and be aware of Gods presence in all things.

Look for God in the small things. The snatched conversation you just had with the shop assistant, God was there; the hug you gave your grieving friend, God was there; the moment you took to smell the flowers, God was there; when you washed up after dinner, God was there. It isn't that God wants to do the washing up for you or promise you that every washing up moment will be filled with joy but God may be telling you that if you spend those times that need little thought, in prayer and conversation with your Creator, then your life may be that bit richer and purposeful.

I should point out that if you don't pray during the washing up your life will not fall apart, I know that sometimes I'm so tired that I can't even form a coherent thought let alone pray sensibly and a few minutes of mindless washing up is a pleasurable chance to switch off. If you can't pray then try singing or humming and just be open to whatever God may want to say to you.

Never 'beat yourself up' for not doing enough, practice just being and be available when God calls you to do something.

Allow yourself to be vulnerable to others and to God. It's not easy to do but when we allow others to see our true selves they will see more of God and God will be able to use you more effectively to help others.